The dragons fly high, breathing fire as they go,
With invitations for friends in the valley below.
There's so much to do, as the ball is tonight,
Decorations to make and lanterns to light.

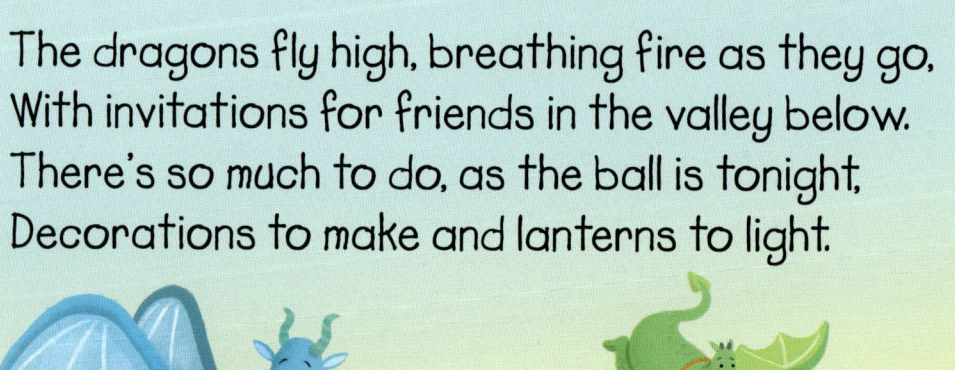

Brownies and sprites bake some great party treats,
Fairy cakes, cookies and more yummy sweets!
Animal friends help them out as they cook,
Finding nuts in the trees and fruit by the brook.

The unicorns search for the best party gift,
But time's running out, so they need to be swift!
The waterfall mermaids offer shiny new pearls,
Then swim away laughing, shaking their curls.

The giants search for glow-worms as twilight falls,
To place inside lanterns and light up castle walls.
As dusk turns to dark, everything's in its place,
And the creatures rush home, a smile on each face!

The fairies dress up before they take flight,
With silky-soft feathers and petals so bright.
The cobwebs they weave into silvery strings,
And delicate nets to decorate their wings.

The castle looks pretty ... a wonderful sight!
And the ball begins at the stroke of midnight.
Magical creatures arrive, one by one,
To sing, laugh and dance ... the party's begun!